WRITE YOUR OWN FUNERAL SERVICE

Prepare and Deliver Your Own
Funeral Service/Celebration of Life for
Family Members, Friends and Loved Ones That
Were Not Able to Receive a Proper Burial Service

© Copyright www.GodLovesYouAndMe.org

Rev. Oreste J. D'Aversa

PUBLISHER'S NOTE

This book is designed to provide accurate and authoritative. information in regard to the subject matter covered. It is sold with the understanding that neither the author nor publisher is engaged in rendering psychological, legal, or other professional service. If psychological, legal, professional advice or other expert assistance is required, the services of a professional, in that field should be sought. The principles and concepts presented in this book are the opinions of the author and based on his interpretations of the aforementioned principles. Neither the author nor publisher is liable or responsible to any person or entity for any errors contained on this book, website, or for any special, incidental, or consequential damage caused or alleged to be caused directly or indirectly by the information contained on this book or website. Any application of the techniques, ideas and suggestions in this book is at the reader's sole discretion and risk.

Copyright © Oreste J. D'Aversa, 2021. All rights reserved.

No part of this publication may be reproduced, redistributed, taught, stored in a retrieval system, or transmitted, in any form, or by any means, electronic, mechanical, photocopy, recording, or otherwise, without the prior written permission of the publisher.

FIRST EDITION

ISBN: 978-1-952294-14-3

Library of Congress Control Number: 2021915355

Published by: Cutting Edge Technology Publishing

The Picture on the Cover – The Phoenix

The Phoenix bird symbolizes immortality, resurrection, and life after death, and in ancient Greek and Egyptian mythology it is associated with the sun god.

Associated with the sun, a phoenix obtains new life by arising from the ashes of its predecessor. Some legends say it dies in a show of flames and combustion, others that it simply dies and decomposes before being born again.

NOTES

Dedication

This book is dedicated to all people who have lost loved ones in their lives without having a chance to say goodbye in a proper, respectful, and loving manner. May your burden be lightened a little and may you find comfort in knowing that the people you love are in a better place and that they send you love in return.

NOTES

Table of Contents

1. About the Author 9
2. Introduction 11
3. Memorial Service 15
4. Funeral Prayers/Quotes 59
5. Conclusion 111
6. Worksheets 113
7. Footnotes 141
8. Bibliography 145

NOTES

1. About the Author

Rev. Oreste J. D'Aversa, "Reverend Rusty" as he is known informally, is an Inter-Faith (All-Faiths) Minister ordained by The New Seminary in New York City, New York.

He believes in the teachings of God, Jesus Christ, the Prophets, and the Ascended Masters. He is here to serve God and humankind to help make the world a better place for all people.

Reverend D'Aversa is an Author, Public Speaker, Spiritual Coach/Advisor and helps people find their true life's purpose and spiritual path. He is also a Business Coach, Consultant, Trainer and University Lecturer. He has appeared on radio and television as well as having his work featured in various newspapers and journals.

He is author of the following books:
- *Life Beyond the Pandemic: A Practical New Journey Handbook*
- *SELLING for NON-SELLING Professionals*
- *Baby Boomer Entrepreneur*
    (all available on Amazon.com)

His websites:
www.GodLovesYouAndMe.org
www.LifeBeyondThePandemic.com
www.MetroSmallBusinessCoaching.com

He can be reached at:
eMail: OresteDAversa@outlook.com

NOTES

2. INTRODUCTION

Whether it is called a **Funeral Service** or a **Celebration of Life** it is a recognition of a person life here on Planet Earth. With all the current life events – the worldwide Pandemic, natural and man-made disasters, many people were and are not able to receive a proper Funeral Service or a Celebration of Life Service. Also, with the aforementioned situations, there may be shortages of Clergy and Funeral Directors to perform a proper Funeral Service or Celebration of Life Service.

I have written this book so that anyone can prepare and deliver a religious and/or spiritual, respectful and professional Funeral Service/Celebration of Life for Family Members, Friends and Loved Ones that have passed away and were not able to receive a proper service.

The book is designed in a simple to read and understand format with **Worksheets** at the end of the book for you to write your own Funeral Service or Celebration of Life Service.

The "Memorial Services Suggested Format" used in this book is a template to perform a service but as mentioned it is only a "Suggested Format". You can use it as is or "keep what you like and leave the rest". Each section will be defined with an example which you can use "as is" or can be modified to fit your needs. Then there is an area where you can write out your specific requirement for that section and at the end of the book there will be blank worksheets where you can put all the sections together to deliver your Funeral Service or Celebration of Life Service. You can take the book with you to deliver the ceremony at a specific location and read your ceremony you have written right out of this book.

What are 7 Purposes of a Funeral Service?
1. **Reality** – to accept the death of a loved one
2. **Acceptance** – the person is longer coming back.
3. **Recall** – to remember the person that has died in a respectful, loving and dignified manner.
4. **Support** – to provide active support to those that have lost someone through the grieving process.
5. **Expression** – to actively express our emotions to help in the healing process.
6. **Meaning** – to find meaning in the person's life and allow ourselves to find peace.
7. **Transcendence** - to helps us find a new self-identity. Funerals help us publicly mark a change in status.

May this guide help you during your time of sorrow and be a healing tool on your spiritual journey through the death of a loved one.

NOTES

3. MEMORIAL SERVICE

Below, as previous mentioned is the **Memorial Service Suggested Format**. It can be used "as is" or as to your specific needs require. You can take out items you feel you do not need, add items that are important to you or rearrange some of the items. The Memorial Service Suggested Format is a starting point to help you write a Funeral Service/Celebration of Life that is appropriate for you, your family, religious/spiritual background and more important appropriate for the person that has died.

I suggest that you write the **Memorial Service** when you are in a calm, reflective and meditative state of mind to express all your thoughts, feelings, and sentiments about the person you are doing the ceremony for. Writing a Memorial Service for an individual is a **sacred duty** to be done for the person that died, the people that knew that person and for GOD as we are all of GOD's creations.

Take your time. Write it out to the best of your ability. Sleep on it and review your Memorial Service to see if you have missed anything or want to add something more to it. If you can't think of anything to write, ask GOD for some suggestions through prayer and meditation and GOD will supply you with what you need to know. If you get really into a jam, you can always go to the internet and ask Mr. Google for some help! 😊

I will go through each item of the **Memorial Service Suggested Format** briefly discuss and/or define it, provide an example, and have a blank area for you to write your own. At the end of the book, you can transfer all of your writings to blank worksheets that you can use, if you wish, to deliver the actual service at any location you choose.

To relieve stress, anxiety, and nervousness about delivering the service, I suggest you practice the service several times out loud to yourself even if it is to an empty room.

Memorial Service Suggested Format

1. Opening Remarks/Introduction/Words of Welcome

2. Prayer of Invocation (Prayer to GOD)

3. Sacred Readings (Scripture, Readings with Special Meaning, Etc.)

4. Prayers

5. Musical Selections/Hymns

6. Formal Reading of Obituary

7. Moments of Silence/Meditation

8. Eulogy/Life Tribute

9. Brief Informal Life Tributes

10. Prayer of Thanksgiving for the Deceased's Life

11. Benediction (short blessing with which public worship is concluded)

12. Thank you and Acknowledgements

13. Closing Remarks

NOTES

1. Opening Remarks/Introduction/ Words of Welcome

Purpose: To begin the Funeral Service/Celebration of Life and welcome attendees.

Sample(s): *"Welcome and thank you all for coming today. We are here today to honor a special person –* **NAME OF PERSON***. No matter how much time I/we had to prepare for this day, I/we still do not feel ready to say goodbye."*

"I/We appreciate how many of you have come to support me/us during this difficult time. Today will not be a traditional funeral service. Instead, we will have a Celebration of Life in honor of the joy **NAME OF PERSON** *brought to so many people."*

1. Opening Remarks/Introduction/ Words of Welcome

2. Prayer of Invocation

Purpose: An invocation prayer is an opening prayer for a service or meeting. Invocation prayers focus on worshipping GOD and seeking His presence in the gathering.

Sample(s): Beloved GOD, I pray that You bless us in the delivery of this Funeral Service/Celebration of Life for **NAME OF PERSON** and keep and protect us. GOD, let Your face shine on us and be gracious to us. We pray that we feel Your presence during this Funeral Service/Celebration of Life because You are with us wherever we go. We pray that this service focuses upon **NAME OF PERSON** well lived life. Amen.

2. Prayer of Invocation (Prayer to GOD)

3. Sacred Readings (Scripture, Readings with Special Meaning, Etc.)

Purpose: Reading from Sacred Texts (The Holy Bible, The Quran, etc.) that have meaning to this Funeral Service/Celebration of Life.

Sample(s): Psalm 23 (The Holy Bible)
The Lord is my shepherd; I shall not want.
²   He makes me lie down in green pastures.
He leads me beside still waters.
³   He restores my soul.
He leads me in paths of righteousness
    for his name's sake.
⁴ Even though I walk through the valley of the shadow of death,
    I will fear no evil,
for you are with me;
    your rod and your staff,
    they comfort me.
⁵ You prepare a table before me
    in the presence of my enemies;
you anoint my head with oil;
    my cup overflows.
⁶ Surely goodness and mercy shall follow me
    all the days of my life,
and I shall dwell in the house of the Lord
    forever.

Oh Soul At Rest, Return To Your Lord (The Quran)

"O soul that are at rest! Return to your Lord, well-pleased (with him), well-pleasing (Him), So enter among My servants, and enter into My garden." (Quran, 89:27-30)

3. Sacred Readings (Scripture, Readings with Special Meaning, Etc.)

4. Prayers (See Chapter 4 for other Prayers)

Purpose: To offer prayers to God on behalf of the person being honored in the Funeral Service/Celebration of Life.

Sample(s): Funeral Blessing for a Loved One

May you always walk in sunshine,

and God's around you flow.

For the happiness you gave us,

No one will ever know.

It broke our hearts to lose you,

But you did not go alone.

A part of us went with you

The day God called you home.

A million times we needed you

A million times we cried.

If love could only have saved you

You would've never died.

The Lord be with you and may you rest in peace.

A Celtic Death Blessing by John O'Donohue

I pray that you will have the blessing of being consoled.

May you know in your soul that there is no need to be afraid.

When your time comes, may you be given every blessing and shelter that you need.

May there be a beautiful welcome for you in the home that you are going to.

You are not going somewhere strange.

You are going back to the home that you never left.

May you have a wonderful urgency to live your life to the full.

May you live compassionately and creatively and transfigure everything that is negative within you and about you.

When you come to die may it be after a long life.

May you be peaceful and happy and in the presence of those who really care for you.

May your going be sheltered and your welcome assured.

May your soul smile in the embrace of your anam cara (soul friend).

4. Prayers

4. Prayers

5. Musical Selections/Hymns

Purpose: Hymns are a meaningful choice of religious **music** that can be played at **funerals**. In addition to bringing peace and comfort for the grieving, **funeral hymns** stir memories strong memories of faith and tradition.

Sample(s): Amazing Grace

Amazing grace
How sweet the sound
That saved a wretch like me
I once was lost, but now I'm found
Was blind, but now I see
'Twas grace that taught my heart to fear
And grace my fears relieved
How precious did that grace appear
The hour I first believed
My chains are gone
I've been set free
My God, my Savior has ransomed me
And like a flood, His mercy rains
Unending love, Amazing grace
The Lord has promised good to me
His word my hope secures
He will my shield and portion be
As long as life endures
My chains are gone
I've been set free (been set free)

My God, my Savior has ransomed me (ransomed me)
And like a flood (like a flood) His mercy rains (mercy rains)
Unending love, oh, Amazing grace
The Earth shall soon dissolve like snow
The sun forbear to shine
But God, Who called me here below
Will be forever mine
My chains are gone
I've been set free
My God, my Savior has ransomed me
And like a flood, His mercy rains
Unending love, Amazing grace (grace)
I once was lost, but now I'm found
Was blind (was blind), but now (but now) I see

Ave Maria

Ave Maria
Gratia plena
Maria, gratia plena
Maria, gratia plena
Ave, ave dominus
Dominus tecum
Benedicta tu in mulieribus
Et benedictus
Et benedictus fructus ventris
Ventris tuae, Jesus.
Ave Maria
Ave Maria
Mater Dei

Ora pro nobis peccatoribus
Ora pro nobis
Ora, ora pro nobis peccatoribus
Nunc et in hora mortis
Et in hora mortis nostrae
Et in hora mortis nostrae
Et in hora mortis nostrae
Ave Maria

English translation:

Hail Mary, full of grace,
Mary, full of grace,
Mary, full of grace,
Hail, Hail, the Lord.
The Lord is with thee.
Blessed art thou among women, and blessed,
Blessed is the fruit of thy womb,
Thy womb, Jesus.
Hail Mary!
Hail Mary, Mother of God,
Pray for us sinners,
Pray, pray for us;
Pray, pray for us sinners,
Now and at the hour of our death,
The hour of our death
The hour of our death,
The hour of our death
Hail Mary.

5. Musical Selections/Hymns

6. Formal Reading of Obituary

Purpose: The obituary, like the funeral service, notifies the public of your loved one's passing. The purpose of an obituary is to notify the public of an individual's passing and relay the details of the services. It can also detail the life of the deceased.

Sample(s):
What Should Be Included?

- Announcement
- Biographical Information
- Survivors and Predeceased Information
- Scheduled Services
- Memorials
- Final Considerations

Obituary Samples

The following are fictitious examples of obituaries:

FORBES, Alex Downton

It is with great sadness that the family of Alex Downton Forbes announces his passing after a brief illness, on Saturday, April 3, 2014, at the age of 70 years. Alex will be lovingly remembered by his wife of 45 years, Joan and his children, Mike (Judy), Brad (Jill), Sue (Dan) Armandeau, and Ryan (Heidi). Bill will also be fondly remembered by his eight grandchildren, Brandy, Kala, Jack, Phillip, Jonah,

Mackenzie, Paul and Austin, by his sisters, Ann (Joe) Kispinski, Eileen Rudolph and by sister-in-law Anne Forbes. Alex was predeceased by his brother Anton Forbes.

A Funeral Service in memory of Alex will be held on Thursday, April 7, 2014 at 1:00 p.m., at the Oliver's Funeral Home, 10005 - 107 Ave, Grande Prairie, with Rev. George Malcolm officiating. Interment will follow in the family plot at Emerson Trail Cemetery. Those who so desire may make memorial donations in memory of Alex to the (name and mailing address of foundation/society).

Riley, Laura (nee Gorman)

On Monday, February 3, 2014, Laura Riley, wife, mother, daughter and sister, passed away suddenly at the age of 36 years. Laura will be forever remembered by her husband and best friend Greg, and their precious children, Cody and Pamela, by her parents Jack and Ann Gorman, and by her brothers and sisters Andrew (Jill), Ken (Hope), Kim (Justin) Halow and Tianna (Wade) O'Halen. Andrea will also be forever remembered by her numerous nieces, nephews and extended family and dear friends.

A Prayer Service will be held on Thursday, February 6, at 7:00 p.m., at Oliver's Funeral Home, 10005 – 107 Ave, Grande Prairie.

A Mass of Christian Burial will be celebrated in memory of Laura on Friday, February 7, at 10:00 a.m., at St. Joseph ' s Catholic Church, 10404 - 102 Street, Grande Prairie, with Reverend Remi Hebert C.Ss.R. presiding.

Memorial donations in memory of Laura may be made to (name and mailing address of foundation/society).

6. Formal Reading of Obituary

7. Moments of Silence/Meditation

Purpose: To reflect in silence the life of the person that has died and to ponder our own lives on Earth.

Sample(s):
The meditation can be quiet time or the pondering of sacred scripture, hymn or anything that will help all attending reflect on the fragility of life and that we occupy this Earth for a short time.

7. Moments of Silence/Meditation

8. Eulogy/Life Tribute

Purpose: A eulogy is a speech given at a memorial service in memory of a person who has died. The purpose is to recall the defining qualities and highlights of a life lived in a way that benefits the audience, particularly the family.

Sample(s): Below is a Eulogy Template

<u>**Eulogy Template**</u>

Introduction

Childhood

Education & Career

Family

Hobbies

Commemorations

Conclusion

EULOGY EXAMPLE

Below is an example of the structure of a Eulogy.

In providing this, we aim to spark your creativity in writing part of the life story of your loved one.

Start off with what is provided below. On the following page you will find a blank template for you to fill in the blanks. Insert the details in brackets of your loved one and add as much extra detail as you like. The short sections provided are launching points to get you going in the right direction.

You may also like to begin or end with one of the scriptures, poems or readings from above.

INTRODUCTION

Today we gather to honor, remember, and say goodbye to (**NAME OF DECEASED PERSON**).

Taking the words of a famous writer: "We make a living by what we get, we make a life by what we give". If that is true, then (name of deceased) made a great life. He was the most generous person I've ever known. I know many of you would agree judging from the nodding heads around the room.

CHILDHOOD

Our lives have all been touched by (**NAME OF DECEASED PERSON**) in some way, but you may not have known some details of their earlier life. (**NAME OF DECEASED PERSON**) was born (**FULL BIRTH NAME**) on (**THEIR BIRTH DATE**) in (**City**). He/She was the (**First, Second, only**) child of (**Name of loved one's Father**) and (**Name of loved one's Mother**). They lived in (**City**) from (**Year**) to (**Year**), and later moved to and (**Town**).

EDUCATION & CAREER

(**NAME OF DECEASED PERSON**) went to (**School**) and (Name of Schools) and graduated with (Name of Degree or Training). While studying at (School) (**NAME OF DECEASED PERSON**) was able to achieve (**List Achievements or Awards**). During this time (**NAME OF DECEASED PERSON**) became good friends with (**List of Friends Names**) and they remained good friends to this day.

He/She then went to work for (**Name of Company**) as a (**Name of Position**). Over the years, (**NAME OF DECEASED PERSON**) also worked for (**Company**), (**Company**) and (**Company**) OR also worked in (**Type of Job**). While working for (**Company**) (**NAME OF DECEASED PERSON**) was able to achieve (**List Achievements or Awards**).

FAMILY

In **(Year)** **(NAME OF DECEASED PERSON)** met **(Name of Spouse)** and they were married **(Number)** years later. Eventually they had **(Number)** children **(Names of their Children)**. Last year, **(NAME OF DECEASED PERSON)** and **(Spouse's Name)** celebrated their **(Number, e.g. 50th)** wedding anniversary.

HOBBIES

(NAME OF DECEASED PERSON) was very active in the **(Church, Community, Local Theatre, Quilting, Volunteer Firefighting)**. He/She devoted many hours to (hobby or service) and was known for **(what person was known for in the hobby or service, e.g. her exquisite quilt designs; always being ready with a helping hand; always having a positive attitude)**.

COMMEMORATIONS

I asked family and friends to tell me what they remember most about **(NAME OF DECEASED PERSON)**. There are so many good memories. **(List 5 or 6 memories in short sentence form, e.g. Playing music together. Fishing. His big hearty laugh. The time we went to Italy)**. One that I remember in particular is the time when **(tell a longer story that illustrates your loved one's** personality – this can be a heart-warming story or a humorous story).

CONCLUSION

(**NAME OF DECEASED PERSON**) was a remarkably (an adjective, e.g. good; thoughtful; hardworking; fun-loving) person. He/She was a person of great (two words that describe the person's character, e.g. devotion, integrity, love, compassion, service, humor).

Above all, (**NAME OF DECEASED PERSON**) believed in (**The person's highest value, e.g. family, faith, hard work, independence, community, compassion**). He/She always said (**A common saying that illustrates the person's highest value, e.g. "family is the most important thing in life"; "you get out of life what you put into it"; "life is short, so enjoy it while you can!"**).

Those are words of wisdom that I will always cherish.

In closing, I would like to share this poem with you:

<Use a poem, reading or scripture from above>

(**NAME OF DECEASED PERSON**), thank you for being part of our lives. We are all going to miss you deeply.

8. Eulogy/Life Tribute

9. Brief Informal Life Tributes

Purpose: Funerals are more about remembering the happy memories with a person who died than about being sad and saying goodbye. A Memorial Tribute helps comfort and may be delivered by friends and family members and support them during their grieving process.

Sample(s):

"The first thing I noticed about Sally was her big blonde, curly hair. It didn't take long to discover that her hair matched her personality. And it's that personality that I would like to celebrate with you today.

Let's start by remembering her laugh. I always knew where Sally was when I entered a restaurant for a lunch date with her and our high school friends. I only had to pause at the entrance of the dining room and listen for her loud, contagious laugh. I never had to wait long to hear it because Sally was always the life of the party."

9. Brief Informal Tributes

10. Prayer of Thanksgiving for the Deceased's Life

Purpose: To give thanks to GOD for the deceased's life.

Sample(s):

Eternal rest grant unto them, O Lord, and let perpetual light shine upon them. May the souls of the faithful departed through the mercy of God rest in peace. Amen.

Dear Heavenly Father, it is always hard to say goodbye to those that have died, for we know that they will be missed by so many who are left behind. But Lord, You also remind us that the death of Your saints is very special to You and we want to join together to thank You for life of this Your child, who was such an encouragement and wonderful witness of Your love and grace.

Thank You, Lord, for the blessings of this special person, whom we all remember so fondly, but who is now at rest in Your loving embrace. Thank You for their life and the many happy memories that we all share.

We pray that You will be a special comfort, to uplift and care for those that will feel the greatest loss. Help us to remember that although we are separated for a time, we will all rejoice one day when we stand together in Your presence. Thank You that the brief night of weeping will pass very quickly, and we will all be rejoicing in Your presence on that glorious morning when we will all be reunited in the hope that is set before us. In Jesus' name we pray,

Amen.

----

10. Prayer of Thanksgiving for the Deceased's Life

NOTES

11. Benediction (short blessing with which public worship is concluded)

Purpose: The short prayer at the end of a funeral service is actually for the funeral leader to pronounce a blessing of God on those attending and to ask for guidance in the days to come. A benediction is an official dismissal.

Sample(s):

"May the Lord bless you and keep you; the Lord make his face shine upon you and be gracious unto you; the Lord turn his face toward you and give you peace."

11. Benediction (short blessing with which public worship is concluded)

12. Thank you and Acknowledgements

Purpose: To show appreciation to all those that help you and your family during the funeral process.

Sample(s):

"Our whole family thanks you all for all of your assistance during this very difficult time. Thank you for your love and very support through everything."

"Thank you, **NAME**, **NAME**, and **NAME**, for the **SPECIFIC THINGS THEY DID** to help our family. It meant a lot to us all and was a very big help."

"**NAME OF DECEASED**" would have loved your flowers, they were perfect. Thank you so much for such a beautiful contribution."

12. Thank you and Acknowledgements

13. Closing Remarks

Purpose: Closing statements in the Funeral Service/Celebration of Life Service

Sample(s):

The **NAME OF DECEASED** family and friends, thank you for joining us as the Saint Michael's community mourns the loss of Robert. Robert was one of the greatest storytellers we will ever know - a Utah voice whose plots and people, while they came to us from small and out-of-the-way places, spoke to all of us, whatever our life experiences. His themes were not limited by time and place - they were about our struggles with choices between good and evil in their everyday manifestations. Robert showed us that we do have choices, and that they are important, no matter how restricted our realm. And with his loving heart, discerning eye and keen sense of humor, Robert made us laugh while we absorbed these serious lessons.

Please join us at the Moonlight Diner for some food and storytelling - something that our beloved friend was a master at.

13. Closing Remarks

Notes

4. Funeral Prayers/Quotes

In this section there will be prayers by religion and spiritual traditions that can be used in your **Memorial Service,** or you can use your own. Some traditions are more a way of life rather than an organized religion, Confucianism, for example. For these types of situations meaningful Quotes will be used from their traditions.

NOTES

a. African Religions [1]

**Praise Ye Lord,
Peace be with us.**

Say that the elders may have wisdom and speak with one voice.
Peace be with us.

Say that the country may have tranquility.
Peace be with us.

And the people may continue to increase.
Peace be with us.

Say that the people and the flock and the herds
May prosper and be free from illness.
Peace be with us.

Say that the fields may bear much fruit
And the land may continue to be fertile.
Peace be with us.

May peace reign over earth,
May the gourd cup agree with vessel.
Peace be with us.

May their heads agree and every ill word be driven out
Into the wilderness, into the virgin forest.

– Kikuyu Peace Prayer –

http://www.godprayers.org/Kikuyu-Peace-Prayer.htm

Great is O King,
our happiness
in thy kingdom,
thou, our king.

We dance before thee,
our king,
by the strength
of thy kingdom.

May our feet
be made strong.
let us dance before thee,
eternal.

Give ye praise,
all angels,
to him above
who is worthy of praise.

– Zulu, South Africa –

http://www.dailyom.com/library/000/000/000000461.html

Agbegi lere, la'fin ewu l'ado,
He who carves the cloth at Ado in the form of a sculpture,

Eiti Olodumare ko pa'jo iku e da,
The one whose date of death
has not been changed by the wind,

Omo Oluworiogbo,
Child of the Chief Priest who made
all the Heads that exist in Creation.

Iba'se ila Oorun,
Homage to the power of East,

Iba'se iwo Oorun,
Homage to the power of the West,

Iba'se Ariwa,
Homage to the power of the North,

Iba'se Guusu,
Homage to the power of the South,

Iba Oba Igbalaye,
Homage to the King of the Seasons of the Earth,

Iba Orun Oke,
Homage to the Invisible Realm of the Mountains,

Iba Atiwo Orun,
Homage to all things that live in the Invisible Realm,

Iba Okiti biri, Oba ti np'ojo iku da,
Homage to the Averter of the final days,
The King who could change the time of Death,

Iba ate-ika eni Olodumare,
Homage to the mat that cannot be rolled up once laid out,

Iba Odemu demu kete a lenu ma fohun,
Homage to the power that extracts Goodness
from the Realm of the Invisible,

Iba'se awon Iku emese Orun,
Homage to the dead, the messengers of the Invisible Realm.

– Iba'se, Parts of the Ifa Prayer of Praise, West Africa –

---

b. Bahá' í Faith [2]

Prayer for the Dead

(The Prayer for the Dead is the only Bahá'í obligatory prayer that is to be recited in congregation; it is to be recited by one believer while all present stand in silence. Bahá'u'lláh has clarified that this prayer is required only when the deceased is over the age of fifteen, that its recital must precede interment, and that there is no requirement to face the Qiblih during its recitation. "Alláh-u-Abhá" is said once; then the first of the six verses is recited nineteen times. Then "Alláh-u-Abhá" is said again, followed by the second verse, which is recited nineteen times, and so on.)

O my God! This is Thy servant and the son of Thy servant who hath believed in Thee and in Thy signs, and set his face towards Thee, wholly detached from all except Thee. Thou art, verily, of those who show mercy the most merciful.

Deal with him, O Thou Who forgivest the sins of men and concealest their faults, as beseemeth the heaven of Thy bounty and the ocean of Thy grace. Grant him admission within the precincts of Thy transcendent mercy that was before the foundation of earth and heaven. There is no God but Thee, the Ever-Forgiving, the Most Generous.

Let him, then, repeat six times the greeting "Alláh-u-Abhá," and then repeat nineteen times each of the following verses:

We all, verily, worship God.

We all, verily, bow down before God.

We all, verily, are devoted unto God.

We all, verily, give praise unto God.

We all, verily, yield thanks unto God.

We all, verily, are patient in God.

(If the dead be a woman, let him say: This is Thy handmaiden and the daughter of Thy handmaiden, etc...)

---

c. Buddhism [3]

1. "Tibetan Dying Prayer"

Through your blessing, grace, and guidance, through the power of the light that streams from you:
May all my negative karma, destructive emotions, obscurations, and blockages be purified and removed,
May I know myself forgiven for all the harm I may have thought and done,
May I accomplish this profound practice of phowa, and die a good and peaceful death,
And through the triumph of my death, may I be able to benefit all other beings, living or dead.

---

2. "A Buddhist Prayer for Peace"

May all beings everywhere plagued with sufferings of body and mind quickly be freed from their illnesses.
May those frightened cease to be afraid, and may those bound be free.

May the powerless find power and may people think of befriending one another.

May those who find themselves in trackless, fearful wildernesses— the children, the aged, the unprotected—be guarded by beneficent celestials, and may they swiftly attain Buddhahood.

3. "Traditional Buddhist Blessing and Healing Chant"

Just as the soft rains fill the streams,
Pour into the rivers and join together in the oceans,
So may the power of every moment of your goodness
Flow forth to awaken and heal all beings,
Those here now, those gone before, those yet to come.

By the power of every moment of your goodness
May your heart's wishes be soon fulfilled
As completely shining as the bright full moon,
As magically as by a wish-fulfilling gem.

By the power of every moment of your goodness
May all dangers be averted and all disease be gone.
May no obstacle come across your way.
May you enjoy fulfillment and long life.

For all in whose heart dwells respect,
Who follow the wisdom and compassion, of the Way,
May your life prosper in the four blessings
Of old age, beauty, happiness, and strength.

d. Christianity [4]

Prayer for the Dead

God our Father,
Your power brings us to birth,
Your providence guides our lives,
and by Your command we return to dust.

Lord, those who die still live in Your presence,
their lives change but do not end.
I pray in hope for my family,
relatives and friends,
and for all the dead known to You alone.

In company with Christ,
Who died and now lives,
may they rejoice in Your kingdom,
where all our tears are wiped away.
Unite us together again in one family,
to sing Your praise forever and ever.

Amen.

Cemetery Prayer # 2

In sure and certain hope of the resurrection to eternal life

through Our Lord Jesus Christ,
we commend to Almighty God **(Name)**,
and we commit his/her body to the ground:
earth to earth,
ashes to ashes,
dust to dust.

The Lord bless him/her and keep him/her,
the Lord make His Face to shine upon him/her
and be gracious to him/her,
the Lord lift up His countenance upon him/her
and give him/her peace.

Amen.

Cemetery Prayer # 3

O God, this hour revives in us memories of loved ones
who are here no more.
What happiness we shared when they walked among us!
What joy, when, loving and loved,
we lived our lives together!
Their memory is a blessing forever.

Months or years may have passed,
yet we feel near to them.
Our hearts yearn for them.
Though the bitter grief has softened,

a duller pain abides,
for the place where once they stood is empty now.
The links of life are broken,
but the links of love and longing cannot break.
Their souls are bound up with ours forever.

O Lord, I thank You
for allowing me to have these very special people in my life.

I have been truly blessed by their presence,
their words and actions, and their love.
I grieve not for them, but for myself, as I truly miss them.
We shared so much,
and yet I feel our times together were fleeting.
Help me, O God,
to realize that the distance between us now
is not so great and that one day,
I will be reunited with them in paradise.
Together, we will glorify You,
Almighty Father, Your only Son, Jesus Christ,
and Your Holy Spirit for all eternity.

Amen.

NOTES

e. Confucianism [5]

Death and life have their determined appointments riches and honors depend upon heaven.

-Confucius

If we don't know life, how can we know death?

-Confucius

Heaven means to be one with God.

-Confucius

NOTES

f. Hinduism [6]

At Hindu funerals, prayers are meant to celebrate the deceased and give comfort to the living. Traditional funeral prayers blend both aspects of life and often combine the recite of Hindu mantras to help those living stay conscious.

ANTYESTI

This traditional rite of passage, literally means "last sacrifice" and is often recited at Hindu funerals.

Burn him not up, nor quite consume him, Agni: let not his body or his skin be scattered,

O all possessing Fire, when thou hast matured him, then send him on his way unto the Fathers.

When thou hast made him ready, all possessing Fire, then do thou give him over to the Fathers,

When he attains unto the life that waits him, he shall become subject to the will of gods.

The Sun receive thine eye, the Wind thy Prana (life-principle, breathe); go, as thy merit is, to earth or heaven.

Go, if it be thy lot, unto the waters; go, make thine home in plants with all thy members.

— Rigveda 10.16

NOTES

g. Islam [7]

ISLAMIC FUNERAL PRAYERS

When someone of Islamic faith passes away, Muslims within the community often gather to offer prayers for the deceased's forgiveness.

SALAT-E-JENAZA OR NAMAZE JENAZA

This prayer is offered in a specific way with a few Takbirs, which literally means "God is greater," every Muslim adult male must perform the funeral prayer upon the death of any Muslim.

The prayer begins with the first takbir of Allaho Akbarby Iman.

Glory be to you Oh Allah, and praise be to You, and blessed is Your name, and exalted is Your Majesty, and there is none to be served besides You.

Then, the Iman says the second takbir of Allaho Akbar.

Oh Allah! Send grace and honor on Mohammad and on the family and true followers of Mohammad just as you sent Grace and Honor on Ibrahim and on the family and his true followers. Surely, you are praiseworthy, the Great."

The Iman Say Allaho Akbar, is the third takbir.

Oh Allah! Forgive of us who are alive and those of who are dead; those of us who are present and those of us who are absent' those of us who are young and those of us who are adults; our males and our females. O 'Allah! Whomsoever You keep alive, let him live as a follower of Islam and whomsoever You cause to die, let him die as a believer.

This ends the Salat-e-Jenaza or namaze Jenaza for adults.

THE FUNERAL PRAYER

If the deceased is an adult, male or female, the following Prayer is recited:

O. Allah, forgive our living ones and our deceased ones and those of us who are present and those who are absent, and our young ones and our old ones and our males and our females.

O Allah those of us whom Thou grantest life, keep them firm on Islam, and those of us whom Thou causest to die, cause them to die in the faith. Deprive us not, O Allah, of the benefits relating to the deceased and subject us not to trial after him.

The particular prayer for a deceased male child:

O Allah make him our forerunner, and make him, for us, a reward and a treasure, and make him for us a pleader and accept his pleading.

Particular prayer for a deceased female child:

O Allah makes her our forerunner, and makes her, for us, a reward and a treasure, and make her for us a pleader and accept her pleading.

NOTES

h. Jainism [8]
Namokar Mantra

(These five salutations evaporate and eradicate negative influences. This is the most sacred and auspicious prayer of all Jaina prayers.

With some versions 'Om' is recited at the beginning of the first four lines.

Notes on pronunciations:
- 'A' is pronounced as 'u' as in 'but'
- 'AA' is a long 'aw' sound as in 'saw')

(OM) NAMO ARIHANTAANAM
I bow to the Jinas (Arhants) the Perfected, yet Embodied Souls, possessed of Infinite Consciousness, Energy
and Happiness;

(OM) NAMO SIDDHAANAM
I bow to the Perfect, Pure (Free of Karmic Attachments), Liberated Souls (Siddhas), those who have attained
Moksha,;

(OM) NAMO AAYARIYAANAM
I bow to the Ascetic Leaders (Aacharyas) of the Jaina Order;

(OM) NAMO UVAJJHAAYAANAM
I bow to the Ascetic Preceptors/Teachers (Upadhyayas);

NAMO LOAE SAVVA SAAHUUNAM

I bow to all the Jaina Ascetics (Monks/Nuns) in the world devoted to Purification of Soul/Self.

ESO PANCHA NAMOKAARO
SAVVA PAAVA PANAASANO
MANGALAANAM CHA SAVVESIM
PADHAMAM HAVAI MANGALAM

Kshamaapanaa Sutra

KHAAMEMII SAVVE JIVAA
SAVVE JIVAA KHAMANTU ME
METTI ME SAVVE BHUESUU
VERAM MAJJHAM
NA KENAI.

I grant forgiveness to all living beings;
and may all of them forgive me.
I have friendship with all living beings;
and hostility toward none.

Words of Assurance

Anyone who recognizes their divine self is a new creation.
The old life has gone; a new life has begun.
Friends, believe in the truth and nature of the indestructible, pure Soul; and be at peace.

Prayer for Sending Forth

Living beings are comprised of two substances: material particles and Soul.
The bodies of living beings are mortal, formed from particles of matter.
And to particles of matter these bodies must return.
This is an inescapable law of nature (or 'of the universe').
The Soul is immortal.
Thus even in death we recognize that life continues, with opportunity for continued and
increased happiness.
May the Soul of _____ be now in a place where there is neither pain nor
sorrow nor dying. Where it can continue to make progress toward Moksha/Liberation; when
there is eternal bliss and forevermore freedom from the suffering of the cycle of birth, death
and rebirth.
Shuddha A–tm–a, Shuddha A–tm–a, Shuddha A–tm–.
Pure Soul, Pure Soul, Pure Soul

NOTES

i. Judaism [9]

Mourner's Kaddish

Kaddish prayers are a cornerstone of Judaism. They provide an opportunity for mourners to praise God's name and acknowledge their pain. The term comes from an Aramaic word which means 'holy.' This praise is obvious in an excerpt of the prayer:

"May His great name be kept magnified and sanctified in the world that is to be created anew, where He will revive the dead, and raise them up to eternal life; and rebuild the city of Jerusalem; and establish His Temple in its midst; and uproot alien worship from the earth and restore the worship of Heaven to its place. May the Holy One, blessed be He, reign in His sovereignty and glory, during your life ring your days."

The Kaddish provides hope. In the Jewish faith, God will resurrect the righteous to experience eternal life. This allows mourners to believe that they will see their loved ones again. The Kaddish also serves as a guide through many complex stages of grief. One of the issues with a Western approach to grief is speed.

Grief makes people uncomfortable. It's hard to cope with. The bereaved 'should' sweep all their emotions under the rug as soon as possible. It's even a subject of praise. Mentioning how 'strong' someone is, or how 'well they're holding up' is common in Western culture.

This can make someone feel like everyone has forgotten the deceased. They may feel that they're expected to move on as if nothing happened. In Judaism, this isn't the case. When a close relative passes away, a Kaddish is recited by mourners for eleven months. This allows a slow transition back into the ordinary world.

El Maleh Rachamim (Jewish Prayer of the Dead)

The phrase 'el maleh rachamim' translates to 'God full of compassion'. Indeed, this prayer is a call to God's compassionate nature. In Jewish thought, souls go to paradise after death.

This prayer pleads with God to give them rest and contentment in the next world. Asking God to have mercy is a tradition in the Jewish faith. An excerpt from the prayer demonstrates this:

"Oh God, full of compassion, who dwells on high, grant true rest upon the wings of the Divine Presence, in the exalted spheres of the holy and pure ... Therefore, may the All-Merciful One shelter him with the cover of His wings forever, and bind his soul in the bond of life. The Lord is his heritage, may he rest in his resting-place in peace; and let us say: Amen."

Psalm 90

The Psalms are a cornerstone of the Jewish liturgy and faith. They express a broad range of emotions. From anger with God to heart-stopping sorrow, to endless joy, the Psalms are a form of human expression. The extent of emotions they discuss is why they are commonly used in funerals.

"My protector, You are our abode, one generation to the next, Since before the mountains came to birth, before the birth pangs of the land and world. From eternity to eternity, You are divine. Truly, a thousand years are in your eyes like yesterday--so quickly does it pass--or like the watchman's nighttime post. You pour upon them sleep, they sleep ... At dawn, life blossoms and renews itself; at dusk, it withers and dries up."

King David, a figure who experienced much personal loss, is said to have written many of these Psalms.

NOTES

j. Native American [10]

Great Spirit Prayer

Oh, Great Spirit,
Whose voice I hear in the winds
and whose breath gives life to all the world.
Hear me! I need your strength and wisdom.
Let me walk in beauty, and make my eyes
ever hold the red and purple sunset.
Make my hands respect the things you have made
and my ears sharp to hear your voice.
Make me wise so that I may understand
the things you have taught my people.
Let me learn the lessons you have hidden
in every leaf and rock.

Help me remain calm and strong in the
face of all that comes towards me.
Help me find compassion without
empathy overwhelming me.
I seek strength, not to be greater than my brother,
but to fight my greatest enemy: myself.
Make me always ready to come to you
with clean hands and straight eyes.
So when life fades, as the fading sunset,
my spirit may come to you without shame.

- Translated by Lakota Sioux Chief Yellow Lark in 1887

Prayer for Life

Our old women gods, we ask you!
Our old women gods, we ask you!
Then give us long life together,
May we live until our frosted hair is white;
May we live till then.
This life that now we know!

- Tewa (North American Indian) Traditional Prayer

A Chinook Prayer

May all I say and all I think
be in harmony with thee,
God within me,
God beyond me,
maker of the trees.

- Chinook prayer, Pacific Northwest Coast

k. Pagan [11]

Funeral Prayers

May your soul take a soft-footed journey,
on a soft-floored path through the old forest
to the Land of Comfort,
where the only tears are the drops of rain falling from leaves,
the only moaning deep ocean swells,
the only sighing light evening breezes.
Rest in that land, with the peace you have earned.

To the person who has died, we say:
"Peace between us; go on your way with our blessing."
To those who have come here for farewells, we say:
"Peace among us; may we live blessed together."

The Goddess

His/her whole life has been like waiting and growing in the womb.
The time has come for his/her birth, from this world into another.
Bring him/her, Goddess, through the pangs of this new birth,
thereinto that other world.
Hold your baby there, draw him/her close to you, feeding him/her
with inexhaustible milk from your ever giving breasts.

Rock him/her in your soothing arms, until he/she knows the peace of a baby resting in his complete faith in his/her mother.

----

1. Shinto [12]

THE PRAYER

A life has ended, with the passing of a friend,
the memories of times, have come to an end,
their threads wove the fabric of an earlier day.

A life has ended, with the passing of a friend,
sunrises and sunsets, bright days and dark nights
circled again and again, and gave context to this life,
moment after moment, their life was lived each day.

A life has ended, with the passing of a friend,
lives have been touched by the dear one's journey,
laughter, tears, hopes, fears, a life has come to an end
memories hold their spirit alive, in my own life.

A life has ended, with the passing of a friend,
the loss of future moments, that will not be,
grateful for moments shared, that nourished me,
moments lived, in casual belief, they would never end.

A part of me has ended, with the passing of a friend,
be they gone from the earthly plane, their spirit soars,
to renew again, in summerland, heaven or another life,
I know not where, but their love remains with me,
for in this life, we friends, did share.

I miss my friend, but they will always be near, inside
of me, inside you, and all who took time to hear,
the music of this life so dear, a life now silent,
living only in the memory, of those who survive.

----

m. Sikhism [13]

Shabads

Shabads are hymns in the Sikh religion. This could refer to the hymns in the Holy Text, the main scripture for Sikhs. It can also be another term for God.

Shabads are commonly read or even sang at funerals. These focus on feelings of hope and healing, so they're powerful for family members. There are no funeral songs, only shabad hymns. While the family could choose their own favorites to read upon the death of a loved one, these are the most common:

- Jeevan Maran Sukh Ho-e
- Jot Milee Sang Jot
- Sooraj Kiran Milae
- Oudhak Samund Salal Kee

Death Prayers

There are many different death prayers recited at the time of death. Prayer plays a significant role in the Sikh tradition and brings families closer to God, from prayers at the dying's bedside to final funeral prayers.

The most common death prayer is the Kirtan Sohila. This is a nighttime prayer in Sikhism. The name itself translates to "Song of

Praise." This is traditionally recited at the end of an evening ceremony, but it's also a standard part of the funeral procession.

Because this is a nighttime prayer, it symbolizes the end of the soul's cycle on Earth, no unlike the sun setting after a long day.

Kirtan Sohila

The bedtime prayer, Kirtan Sohila is usually recited just before sleeping at night. It's name means 'Song of Peace'. Kirtan Sohila is composed of five hymns, the first three by Guru Nanak Dev, the fourth by Guru Ram Das and the fifth by Guru Arjan Dev. This hymn is usually recited at the conclusion of evening ceremonies at the Gurdwara and also recited as part of Sikh funeral services.

Gauri Dipaki Measure, Guru Nanak

God is only One, He is obtained by the Grace of the True Guru.

In whatever house (state of mind) meditation on God is practiced and His praises are snug,

Sing His praises and meditate upon Him in that house.

You, please, sing the praises of my God, the Fearless.

I am a sacrifice to the Song which gives perpetual peace.

Every day, God looks after and beholds all the beings.

None can assess the price of Your Gifts, so how can the Giver be assessed?

The day and hour of the marriage (departure to the next world) is fixed, so the friends should pour the customary oil on the threshold.

Bless the bride, so that union with the Master, may be obtained.

Such calls and summons to reach the next world are sent to every house, every day.

Nanak reminds: meditate on the One, Who sends calls; that day will come soon.

Asa Measure, Guru Nanak

There are six shastras (books of Hindu thought), their six authors and six methods of teaching;

But One God alone is the Teacher of teachers, though He manifests Himself in many ways.

O God! by that religious books way by which your praises are sung is the best,

Follow that way, which glorifies God.

Just as seconds, minutes, hours, quarters of a day, lunar days, week days, months,

Are created by one sun and so are created many seasons by it,

Similarly God, Who is One has many manifestations, so says Nanak.

Dhanasri Measure, Guru Nanak

The sky is the salver; the sun and the moon the lamps; the stars, with their orbs, are the studed pearls.

The fragrance of sandalwood is the incense, the wind the fan and all vegetation are flowers.

Thus Your Wonderful Worship is performed my God! O, the Destroyer of Fears, this is Your true worship with true lamps.

The Unstruck Melody rings and the Divine Music of the Shabad (Word) is the tender flute.

Your eyes are thousands, yet You have no eye; Your forms are thousands, yet You have no form.

Your pure feet are thousands, yet You have no feet; You are without nose, yet You have a thousand noses; Your plays have, in this way, bewitched me.

The same Light pervades all.

This Light causes the light to shine within all.

Through the Gurus advice the divine Light becomes visible.

That, which pleases Him, constitutes His real worship.

My soul bewitched by the Lotus Feet (Divine Hymns) of God, as sweet as honey, for which I am thirsty day and night.

Nanak says: Give the water of Your Mercy to this pied cuckoo, so that I may merge in Your Name.

Gauri Purbi Measure, Guru Ram Das

Lust and anger completely fill this town body; but these have been smashed to pieces by meeting the Saint (Guru).

I have met the Guru, because of my predestined luck and I have intered the sphere of Gods Love.

Salute the True saint with folded hands, this is a great virtuous act.

Lie prostrate before Him, this is a great virtuous act.

Lovers of mammon do not enjoy the taste of Gods Elixir, as within them there is the thorn of ego.

When they walk forward, that thorn pricks them more and more severly; they suffer greater pain and finally receive on their heads, the blows from deaths staff.

True devotees are absorbed in Gods Name, and fear of the pain of birth and deaths leaves them.

They are united with the Everlasting God and gain great honour in the various regions and universes.

O God! the Greatest of the great, save us, we are poor and humble.

Nanak says: the Name is the Sustainer and support of the mortal, and gives Supreme Joy and peace.

Gauri Purbi Measure, Guru Arjan Dev

My friend, I request you that this is the opportune time to serve the saints.

Earn divine profits in this world and live in peace and comfort in the next one.

Life is shortening day and night.

O mind, meet the Guru and set right your affairs.

This world is engrossed in sins and evils; but Gods Divines will swim across it.

He, who is awakened by God, drinks the Nectar of Name and comes to realise the Ineffable God.

Purchase the commodity, for which you have come in this world, and then God will come to reside in your heart with the Gurus Grace.

You will easily obtain your Real Home and will not suffer transmigration.

O Searcher of hearts and Fulfiller of desires! kindly fulfil my hearts desires.

Nanak says: I, your servant, pray that I may become the dust of the Saints feet join the society of saints.

NOTES

n. Taoism [14]

Taoist Prayers

Prayers inspired by those who practice the religious or philosophical tradition of living with the Tao or "The Way."

Disciples of Life

We are born gentle and weak. At death we are hard and stiff. Green plants are tender and filled with sap. When they die they are withered and dry. Therefore the stiff and unbending are the disciples of death. The gentle and yielding are the disciples of life.

- Lao Tzu from the "Tao Te Ching"

Lao-tsu's Peace Prayer

If there is to be peace in the world,
There must be peace in the nations.

If there is to be peace in the nations,
There must be peace in the cities.

If there is to be peace in the cities,
There must be peace between neighbors.

If there is to be peace between neighbors,

There must be peace in the home.

If there is to be peace in the home,
There must be peace in the heart.

- Lao-tsu

Balance Prayer

Lord, let us empty of all doctrines,
The Tao is wisdom eternally inexhaustible.
Fathomless for the mere intellect,
The Tao is the law wherewith all things come into being.

It blunts the edges of the intellect,
Untangles the knots of the mind,
Softens the glare of thinking,
And settles the dust of thought.

Transparent yet invisible,
The Tao exists like deep pellucid water.
Its origin is unknown,
For it existed before Heaven and Earth.

- Lao-tsu

---

o. Zoroastrianism [15]

Funeral (Geh Saania) Ceremony:

At the service and while at the funeral home, a table holding a Iit deevo, the picture of Zarathustra, and flowers may be kept. On a separate table or area, photographs of the deceased during his/her UK time may be appropriate. Some may also prefer playing somber music during the wake or before the funeral service begins. The main part of the ritual of the funeral ceremony is known as Geh Saarna meaning chanting of the Gathas. The Gathas are a set of live divinely inspired hymns composed by prophet Zarathustra. They contain the simple and universal teachings of the Zarathushti religion. The main content of the Geh Saarna prayer is the chanting of the Ahunavaiti Gatha (first of the five Gathas in the ancient language of Avesta. The Ahunavaiti Gatha is recited to comfort and soothe the Soul in the initial stage of its journey to the spiritual world. A Iit deevo (oil lump) or candle is kept on a table near the head side of the casket. Two priests generally perform this ceremony: however, if priests are not available, the ceremony can be performed by any Zarathushti. The two people performing the ceremony cleanse their hands and face with water and complete the Kushti ritual. They then stand a few feet from the body holding two ends of a clean piece of white cloth to maintain paiwand. This implies a close spiritual connection between them and symbolizes a Joint effort with increased strength of the recitation of the prayers.

The translations of some selected verses from the Ahunavaiti Gatha are presented below:

(From the book titled The Teachings of Zarathushtra The Prophet of Iran on How to Think and Succeed in life by T.R. Sethna)

Ha (Chapter) 28 Verse 1:

With uplifted hands and deep humility. I beseech, O Mazda, first and foremost this, the abiding joy of Spenta Mainyu, your holy mind. Grant that I perform all actions in harmony with righteousness (Your Divine Law), and acquire the wisdom of the good mind so that I may bring happiness to the Soul of the Universe.

(The above verse is recited at the start of the first Ha and at the end of each of the seven Has of the Ahunavad Gatha).

Ha (Chapter) 28 Verse 2:

O Ahura Mazda, may I reach you in fullness of knowledge. through good mind, to be graced with realization of both the selves, the physical (lower) self and the mental (higher) self which comes from following your divine law, through which you lead all devotees into the abode of light (Heaven).

Ha (Chapter) 28 Verse 3:

I shall weave songs of adoration, as was never done before for you O Righteousness, and for you O Good Mind, and for you O Mazda Ahura, for through you flourishes divine wisdom and the never waning moral courage. So descend. O Powers, in answer to these invocations and grant us Perfect Bliss.

Ha (Chapter) 28 Verse 4:<.H4>

In truth when singing your praise. I shall attune my Soul to good thoughts and become aware of the blessings which flow from holy deeds undertaken for Mazda Ahura's sake. As long as I have the will and strength, so long I will teach mankind to strive for righteousness.

Ha (Chapter) 29 Verse 11:

When would I attain righteousness, good thoughts and moral courage? O Mazda, on account of equity, ennoble this great brotherhood. O Ahura, we need your blessings for our protection.

Ha (Chapter) 30 Verse 1:

Now I shall proclaim to those who have assembled here, all that is to be learned from Mazda, viz., the hymns of the Lord, the praises of good mind and what noble principled righteousness is, which by its light points out the real bliss.

Ha (Chapter) 30 Verse 2:

Hear the best (Truth) with your ears and decide by your pure mind. Let everybody judge for his own self and find out what he ought to do. Before the great trial let all wake up to this my counsel.

Ha (Chapter) 30 Verse 9:

And may we be like those who have prospered the world, chosen righteousness and the brotherhood of Ahura Mazda. May mind and heart turn in unison to You whenever our reason is overwhelmed with doubt.

Ha (Chapter) 31 Verse 4:

Ahura Mazda, in order that righteousness may be ideal to live for. I desire the excellent divine wisdom, the best of good thoughts and the mighty moral courage with whose help I would overcome untruth.

Ha (Chapter) 33 Verse 12:

Reveal yourself within me. O Ahura, and through divine wisdom grant me desire for perfection through your devotion, O Mazda, grant me goodness as reward for prayers, through righteousness the full vigor of Soul and all embracing love through good thoughts.

Ha (Chapter) 34 Verse 15:

Therefore, O Mazda, you teach me the noblest words and deeds by which I may in truth fulfill my earnest desire of my prayers, achieving it through the good mind and righteousness, O Ahura, through your power (Moral Strength) regenerate my life as you wish it is true.

At the conclusion of the prayers, family members or friends may address the congregation if the family so desires. The congregation pays their last respects and the casket is removed to the disposal site. In North America, cremation is the preferred mode of disposal of the body. The mode of burial is considered to contaminate the earth, is therefore deemed undesirable. It is customary to consign the ashes from the cremation back to nature. In the US, after the funeral service the body in the casket is carried by Funeral Personnel or by family members and friends to the hearse and driven to the cremation site. A funeral procession with cars (head lights on) follows the hearse. At the crematorium the person is given his/her last respects and the priests pray final Kusti prayers and Sarosh Baj. The body is then handed over to the crematorium personnel who then process it for cremation. In the USA close relatives and friends return to the home of the deceased to comfort the family. Before entering the house, Parsis wash their hands and sprinkle water as a ceremonial bath and do their Kusti prayers.

Refreshments may be served for the guests attending the services. According to Parsi customs, relatives and friends avoid eating meal for three days. On the fourth day, the Uthamna ceremony is performed when the Soul is judged and passes over to the other world.

NOTES

5. Conclusion

I hope this guide was helpful in preparing a Funeral Service/Celebration of Life Ceremony for the special person/people in your life.

Hopefully you found the Memorial Service Suggested Template, Prayers/Quotes and Worksheets useful in putting together a meaningful, respectful and professional Funeral Service/Celebration of Life Ceremony.

As previously mentioned, the book is designed in a simple to read and understand format with Worksheets at the end of the book for you to write your own Funeral Service or Celebration of Life Service.

As to not be overwhelmed when writing/preparing the Funeral Service/Celebration of Life Ceremony, if time permits, I suggest you write some of the service, take a break and/or sleep on it and look at it with a "fresh set of eyes" the next day. Should you get overwhelmed by any of this – take a break, get some fresh air and never forget God is always there for help. Never forget, God will find a way where there appears to be no way...

I sincerely hope this guide helps you through your journey at a difficult time in your life.

My GOD bless you and send you, your family and friends' strength, comfort and love!

NOTES

6. WORKSHEETS

NOTES

Memorial Service
(Blank Worksheets)

1. Opening Remarks/Introduction/Words of Welcome

_____

_____

_____

_____

_____

_____

_____

_____

_____

_____

2. Prayer of Invocation (Prayer to GOD)

3. Sacred Readings (Scripture, Readings with Special Meaning, Etc.)

4. Prayers

5. Musical Selections

6. Formal Reading of Obituary

7. Moments of Silence/Meditation

8. Eulogy/Life Tribute

9. Brief Informal Life Tributes

10. Prayer of Thanksgiving for the Deceased's Life

11. Benediction (short blessing with which public worship is concluded)

12. Thank you and Acknowledgements

13. Closing Remarks

Memorial Service
(Blank Worksheets)

1. _____

_____

_____

_____

_____

_____

_____

_____

_____

_____

_____

_____

_____

2.

3.

4.

5.

6.

7.

8.

9.

10.

11.

12.

13.

7. Footnotes

4. Prayers

a. African Religions [1]

Africa Prayers for the Dead

https://tersiaburger.com/2013/10/19/africa-prayers-for-the-dead/

----

b. Bahá'í Faith [2]

Prayer for the Dead

https://www.bahaiprayers.org/depart1.htm

----

c. Buddhism [3]

3 Short Buddhist Prayers for the Dead, Dying or Sick

https://www.joincake.com/blog/buddhist-prayer-for-the-dead/

----

d. Christianity [4]

Prayers for the Dead

https://www.catholic.org/prayers/prayer.php?p=805

e. Confucianism [5]

MeaningIn.com

https://meaningin.com/confucius/death/quotes

---

f. Hinduism [6]

HINDU FUNERAL PRAYERS

https://www.thegardens.com/traditional-funeral-prayers/

---

g. Islam [7]

ISLAMIC FUNERAL PRAYERS

https://www.thegardens.com/traditional-funeral-prayers/

THE FUNERAL PRAYER

https://amjfuneralservices.ca/54/The-Funeral-Prayer.html

---

h. Jainism [8]

India (Jainism)

https://cog.org/wp-content/uploads/2015/10/India-Jainism.pdf

---

i. Judaism [9]

10 Popular Jewish Funeral Prayers and Poems

https://www.joincake.com/blog/jewish-funeral-prayers/

---

j. Native American [10]

JesuitResource.org

https://www.xavier.edu/jesuitresource/online-resources/prayer-index/native-american

---

k. Pagan [11]

A Book of Pagan Prayer

https://documents.pub/download/a-book-of-pagan-ritual-prayerpdf

---

l. Shinto [12]

Prayers.co.uk

https://www.prayers.co.uk/shinto/death-prayer2.html

---

m. Sikhism [13]

Sikh Funerals (Antam Sanskar): Customs, Attire & What to Expect

https://www.joincake.com/blog/sikh-funeral/

Sikhs.org

https://www.sikhs.org/transl6.htm

---

n. Taoism [14]

JusuitResource.org

https://www.xavier.edu/jesuitresource/online-resources/prayer-index/taoist-prayers

---

o. Zoroastrianism [15]

Zoroastrian Rituals and Geh Saarnaa Prayer

http://www.avesta.org/ritual/geh_sarnu.htm

---

8. BIBLIOGRAPHY

Most Sacred Texts of Major World Religions
Religions Most Sacred Text(s)

Religions	Most Sacred Text(s)
Baha'i	The Seven Valleys and The Four Valleys
Buddhism	Tipitaka
Christianity	Christian Bible
Hinduism	The Vedas and The Upanishads
Islam	The Quran and The Hadiths
Jainism	The Agamas
Judaism	The Tanakh and The Talmud
Shintoism	Kojiki
Sikhism	Guru Granth Sahib
Taoism	Tao Te Ching
Wicca	The Book of Shadows
Zoroastrianism	The Avesta

NOTES

www.ingramcontent.com/pod-product-compliance
Lightning Source LLC
Chambersburg PA
CBHW072020110526
44592CB00012B/1387